El Pacific MIYISA BINAGHA

INTERCONNECTING REMOTE SITES OVER THE INTERNET USING A DMVPN NETWORK

El Pacific MIYISA BINAGHA

INTERCONNECTING REMOTE SITES OVER THE INTERNET USING A DMVPN NETWORK

ScienciaScripts

Imprint

Cover image: www.ingimage.com

This book is a translation from the original published under ISBN 978-620-3-42845-2.

Publisher:
Sciencia Scripts
is a trademark of
Dodo Books Indian Ocean Ltd. and OmniScriptum S.R.L publishing group

120 High Road, East Finchley, London, N2 9ED, United Kingdom
Str. Armeneasca 28/1, office 1, Chisinau MD-2012, Republic of Moldova, Europe
Managing Directors: Ieva Konstantinova, Victoria Ursu
info@omniscriptum.com

Printed at: see last page
ISBN: 978-620-8-56158-1

DEDICATION

To My Family.

ACKNOWLEDGEMENTS

Our thanks go firstly to Almighty God, who has been with us right up to the present day and has supported us throughout this period of training and the realisation of our project.

We take this opportunity to thank our family for their great moral and spiritual support, our father, Rev. KASEREKA LUSENGE Joshua, and my dear brothers and sisters. May the grace of God be abundantly granted to them. Our sincere thanks to the Permanent Executive Secretariat of the Geomatics Centralisation Office, through its Permanent Secretary, Ir. Cart. NGENDABAKANA Fréderic for his approval and facilitation of our internship at the Geomatics Centralisation Office. Our sincere thanks to our Head of Department and Editor, KAPITA MUBAKILAY Christian, for his guidance and assistance and for his patience in enabling us to complete our academic training. We would like to thank the Université Espoir d'Afrique in general, through the Rector, for our training and particularly our Chaplain for his moral and spiritual support, but also all the teachers for the training they gave us during our studies. Our thanks go to our teacher and supervisor, MSc. Ir. NIYONGABO Julius for all the time he devoted to us, for his support and for the many pieces of advice he constantly gave us to improve our work. Our thanks also go to the Principal Network Administrator of the Ministry of Finance, Ir. HABONIMANA AUBIN Teddy for his supervision during the course.

We can't finish without thanking all our colleagues, friends and others who have contributed one way or another to the success of this project. Only God, who provides everything, will know how to reward you for the great service you have given us.

TABLE OF CONTENTS

FOREWORD

The world of technology is constantly surprising us with new developments and discoveries in the field of new information and communication technologies. These days, we have more of an advantage than in years gone by, as it is becoming easier and easier to access the Internet from anywhere at any time. Information and communication technology now covers even the remotest corners of the earth in Third World countries, where people are able to connect to the Internet and communicate around the world just as they do in developed countries.

Thanks to the Internet, companies are now able to communicate with their branches, suppliers, customers and partners from anywhere in the world at any time and with a minimum of equipment.

Most companies have a strong need to interconnect their various remote sites to a main site, but also remote sites to each other, while taking communication security into account.

During the work placement we had the privilege of familiarising ourselves with the network and the various technologies that make up the computer system. We put into practice certain theories studied at university but never put into practice until now and discovered new network practices to enrich our professional experience.

This work will serve as a reference to determine the reasons for and importance of securing networks via VPN in the world of telecommunications, and which VPN technology is favourable for large companies wishing to interconnect their remote sites.

CHAPTER I
INTRODUCTION GENERAL

Our internship lasted two months, including 8 weeks, and took place from 16 October to 15 December 2017 at the Permanent Executive Secretariat of the Geomatic Centralisation Office, managed by the Second Vice-Presidency, in the Ministry of Finance Building. This work presents in detail the activities we were able to carry out throughout our internship. During this work placement we had the privilege of familiarising ourselves with the network of the entire Ministry of Finance building, which has 7 levels, and the different technologies that make up the IT system of each department in the building.This course has enabled us to put into practice some of the theories we studied at university but never put into practice until now. This proved to be a very enriching experience for us as professionals, as it enabled us to find out more about the world of work. certain practices in the professional world of our field. Thanks to this internship, we were able to go out into the field to install networks and we got an idea of the responsibility of an engineer in the field of telecommunications. The aim of this report is to present the activities carried out during the work placement and to show the new techniques we have learnt in order to deepen our knowledge in the field of networks. Firstly, we will explain how our academic training has been useful to us throughout our work placement. Secondly, we will present the company in which we carried out my work placement and describe the activities carried out, concluding with a small project that we had to carry out at the end of our work placement.

Preparation through training at the Université Espoir d'Afrique During our training at the Université Espoir d'Afrique(UEA) in the Faculty of Engineering and Technology(IT), Department of Telecommunications Engineering and Management(GGT) in baccalaureate programme since January 2015; we have had the privilege learning courses and assimilating knowledge on the basis of which our title of engineer in this field will be founded. Our academic career has been a long one and is due to end with an internship and a final thesis in the same field.

The University has done its best to provide us with quality training to prepare us for the challenges of the professional world in our field. During our first year, we had to learn the basic courses to acquire a basic understanding of computers and telecommunications networks, as well as general courses for our personal development and calculation courses to prepare us to tackle more complex problems; given that this was a new course for us who had come from secondary school, some of us were unable to adapt and were forced to drop out before the end of the year.

The second year was a year where we now had to enter the field with courses in computer science, programming and networks; we had really been trained and pushed to do research in our field to acquire additional knowledge;

Before the end of the year, we each had to choose a speciality from among the two concentrations in the Telecommunications Engineering and Management (GGT) department, including Mobile Network and Service (MNS) and Systems and Network Security (SNS). We had the privilege of specialising in the Systems and Network Security (SSR) concentration, from the beginning of our specialisation in the second year to the end in the third year, we had to focus on mastering the concepts of networks in depth and we added securing computer systems and networks through classroom lessons, in-depth research but also projects to deepen our speciality. We were privileged to have the best teachers who taught us everything we needed to know to help us face the professional world without fear.

The reason for doing the internship specifically at the Bureau de Centralisation Geomatics

Nature of the Company

The Government took the decision to set up a National Geomatics Centre (CNG), which later became the BCG, with the aim of establishing a Geomatics Office, implementing the platform for data exchange between different ministries, and disseminating orthophotoplans, which constitute the basic reference framework for building up the various layers of basic information (topographic layers) as well as most of the "business" layers (thematic layers) developed by ministries, public institutions, international organisations and private offices. (http://www.sp-bcg.gov.bi/)

Activities of l'Entreprise

- To formulate proposals to the supervisory authority for better coordination of the players involved in the development of the Geographic Information System (GIS);
- Consolidate, archive and manage geographical information from ministries and other institutions in order to build a national GIS;
- Manage the sharing and dissemination of data by signing agreements between the Office and the various user departments and ensure compliance with the terms set out in the agreements;
- To provide advisory support to other partners involved in the geographic information system in partnership with the University of Burundi or any other research institution with recognised GIS expertise;
- Drawing up specifications for partner institutions' products, in particular the acquisition methodology, file format and projections;
- Ensuring that the standards established for the various layers of geographic

information making up the national GIS are maintained, particularly as regards file formats, projections, organisation and nomenclature;

- Carry out product quality control, ensuring compliance with specifications and established standards before distribution to other institutions;
- Manage the metadata entered for each layer of information or product supplied;

- Drawing up a data catalogue, updating and publishing it. (http://www.sp-bcg.gov.bi/)

The motivation behind our decision to do the internship in the field of Networks

During our training at the Université Espoir d'Afrique(UEA) in the Faculty of Engineering and Technology(IT), Department of Telecommunications Engineering and Management(GGT) in the Systems and Network Security(SSR) speciality, we had to acquire theoretical knowledge and simulate certain configurations and designs in several projects. At the same time, the need to be able to materialise our projects and make configurations on physical equipment was stronger for us. The aim of the end-of-study work placement is to give students an insight into the professional world, and our choice of the networks field will enable us to put all the theoretical knowledge we have into practice and build on the knowledge we have acquired throughout our academic career. This internship is an opportunity for us to familiarise ourselves with the equipment and learn practical techniques to give us the ability to face the professional world in our field.

CHAPTER II

DESCRIPTION OF THE COMPANY AND ITS ACTIVITIES

Detailed presentation of l'Entreprise

Background Preparatory activities

GIS platform (2010-2012): Since 2011, a national GIS platform coordinated by the Second Vice-President of the Republic of Burundi, the Centre National de Coordination des Aides (CNCA), has been initiated: it has enabled the start of national consultation and reflection activities, experience sharing and awareness-raising among national stakeholders. (http://www.sp-bcg.gov.bi/)

GIS study (2011-2012): At the same time, an expert mission, funded by the EU via the Post-Conflict Sustainable Development Programme (PPCDR), was mobilised to carry out (i) a diagnosis of what already existed in terms of GIS, (ii) to draw up a short-term action plan for setting up a National GIS and (iii) to propose various institutional arrangements implementing the National GIS. On the basis of this expertise, the Government decided to set up a National Geomatics Centre (CNG), which subsequently became the BCG. Following this decision, the experts drafted (iv) an "Institutional set-up" report setting out the details of the implementation of this system. (http://www.sp-bcg.gov.bi/) In addition, to facilitate the creation of the Geomatics Office and the implementation of the data exchange platform, dedicated technical assistance (TA) has been mobilised since November 2012. Two national workshops were organised, the first in July 2011 and the second in May 2012. These two workshops resulted in a national consensus for the institutional set-up of the proposed INDS, as well as the drafting of a 1st action plan. (http://www.sp-bcg.gov.bi/)

Creation of the Geomatic Centralisation Office and initial activities

In November and December 2012, the decree creating the BCG was defended in the Council of Ministers, which led to the signing on 9 January 2013 of decree 100/06 creating the Geomatic Centralisation Office. During the first half of 2013, a human resources development plan was developed and implemented: The BCG team has been at work since 11 March 2013. (http://www.sp-bcg.gov.bi/)

Missions

The Permanent Executive Secretariat of the Geomatics Centralisation Office is responsible implementing the OCG's policy and strategic guidelines. More specifically, its roles are to

- orchestrating the development of Burundi's National Spatial Data Infrastructure (INDSB).
- coordinate the activities of the various public institutions in the field of geomatics;
- managing information flows in accordance with the data exchange and sharing agreements signed with the various institutions.

Organisation Institutional set-up

The BCG is made up of a Steering Committee (SC), a Permanent Executive Secretariat and a network of partners. (http://www.sp-bcg.gov.bi/)

Figure 1.B.1 BCG organisation chart

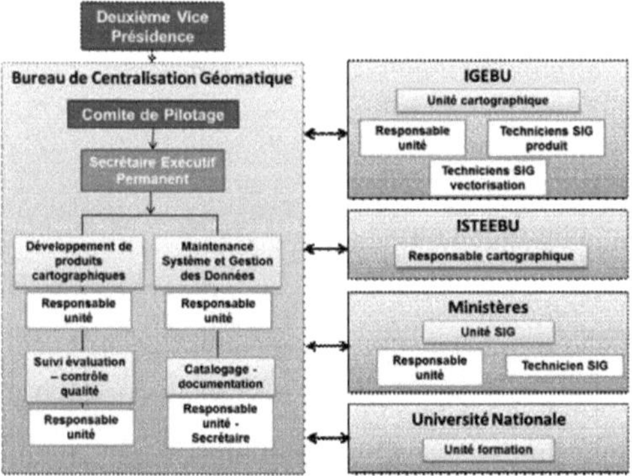

Source : http://www.sp-bcg.gov.bi/

Steering committee

The steering committee is made up of the following members:

Chairman:

Second Vice-President of the Republic

Vice-Chairman :

Minister for Water, the Environment, Town and Country Planning and Urban Development

Members :

1. Minister for the Interior

2. Minister for Economic Development Planning

3. Minister for Public Health

4. Minister for Higher Education and Scientific Research

5. Minister for Agriculture and Livestock

6. Minister for Energy and Mines

7. Managing Director of ISTEEBU

8. Managing Director of IGEBU

9. Permanent Executive Secretary of the BCG (Secretary)

Geographical location

The Permanent Executive Secretariat of the Geomatic Centralisation Office is located in the Building of the Ministry of Finance, 3rd Floor; Boulevard du Japon; RN3; Bujumbura- Mairie; Bujumbura Burundi. (http://www.sp-bcg.gov.bi/)It is bounded to the north by Avenue du Palmier, to the south by Avenue du Manguier, to the east by Avenue de la Révolution and to the west by Boulevard de la Liberté.

Official website

http://www.sp-bcg.gov.bi/

Description of activities

Description of the Ministry of Finance Network

Figure 2.B.1 Presentation of the Ministry of Finance Network

Source: IT Department of the Ministry of Finance of the Republic of Burundi

The Ministry of Finance's network covers a seven-storey building, with each office having at least three network sockets.The server room, which is also the room that links the internal network to the external network, is located on the second floor in room 2-31 and contains, among other things :

A main router for connections to the outside world and a backup router, all Cisco 2900series routers connected to the Core-Switch; A Core-Switch Data which is the coupling of two Switches put together; ONATEL equipment for the fibre optic connection which leads directly to the Core-Switch; Cisco telephones, network photocopiers, Switches and access points.

Each floor pulls the cables from the Core-Switch through the sockets on the wall in the server room.

Figure 3.B.1 Connection between sockets and Core-Switch

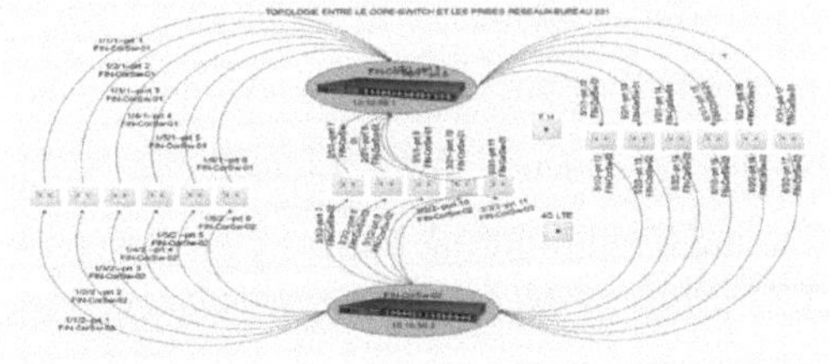

Source: IT Department of the Ministry of Finance of the Republic of Burundi

The server room houses a KVM switch and a KVM screen for server management. It should be noted that this server switch is connected via fibre optics. In each Technical Room there are RACs to house network equipment. The figure below shows an RAC with a KVM screen.

Figure 4.B.1 RAC with KVM screen

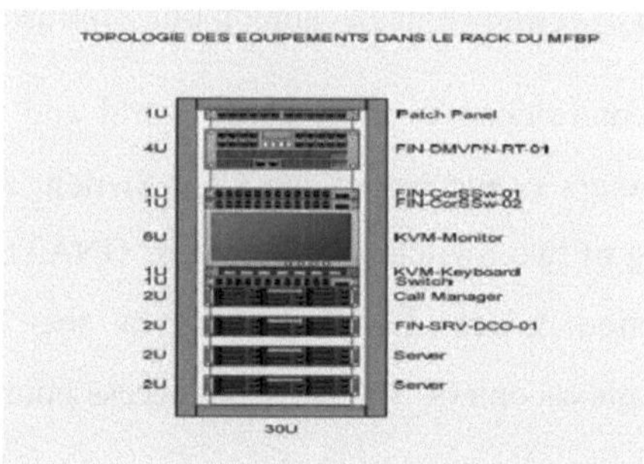

Source: IT Department of the Ministry of Finance of the Republic of Burundi

It should also be noted that this network is a redundancy for that of the Presidency, which is the main site for the WAN network of all government institutions in Burundi. It also includes a Mikrotik router for managing antennas and software for managing hotspot controllers. All the institutions are linked to each other and to the Presidency by connections, with all the antennae connected directly to the small Mikrotik router in the server room.

Figure 5.B.1 Radio links between all government institutions

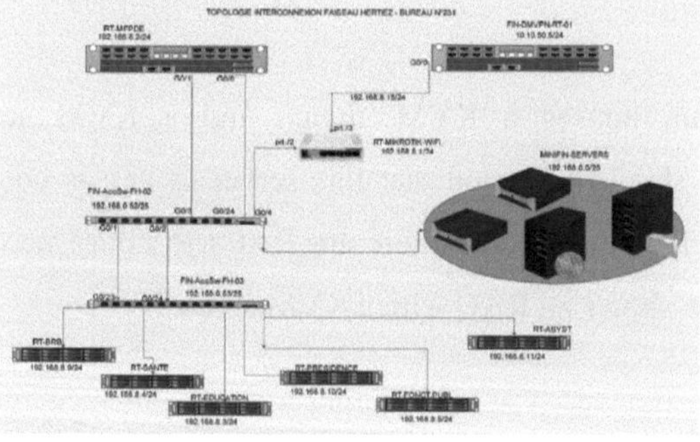

Source: IT Department of the Ministry of Finance of the Republic of Burundi

There are many servers here, including application, production and antivirus servers, the server manages DHCP, DNS and Active Directory, as well as a NAS (Network Administration Storage Server) backup server, and there is a fibre optic connection from BBS, ONATEL and LUMITEL. All users are in the gov.local domain, with the scope for IPv4 DHCP VLANs fin-srv-dc0-01.gov.local; all Burundi ministries share the Active Directory with the Presidency, but have their own DHCP. PRTG Network Monitor software is used to monitor the entire network; all Cisco switches and routers are managed by Secure CRT software; antivirus software is managed by Symantec Endpoint Protection Manager software; and Edraw Max is used for topology. Our security policy requires us to change all the passwords for the entire network every 45 days.

Figure 6.B.1 Server room network topology

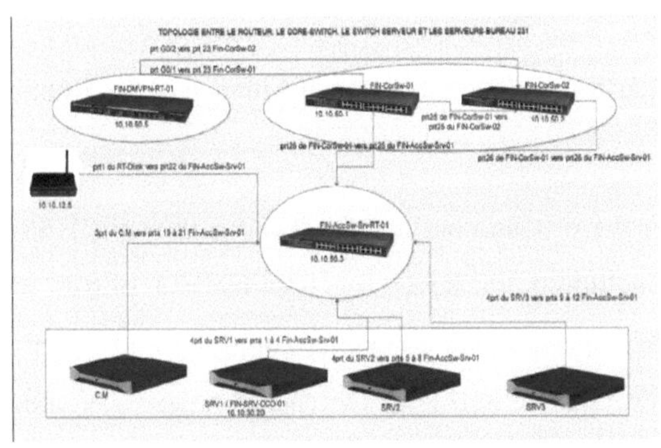

Source: IT Department of the Ministry of Finance of the Republic of Burundi

Each level has a technical room containing all the connections from the server room to the offices on that level. On the ground floor, in room G-24, we have the first technical room of our network: Two RACs, one for telephony and ONATEL fibre optics and another for all the other connectivities on this level. A Fibre Distribution Frame for the optical fibre; a BBS Switch, a PoE Switch that connects the telephones directly, data Switches and panel patches; We also find in this technical room, a 220v power quiet emergency power connected to the generator. It is very important to note that the room is air-conditioned to cool the equipment.

Figure 7.B.1 Ré-des-chaussées network topology

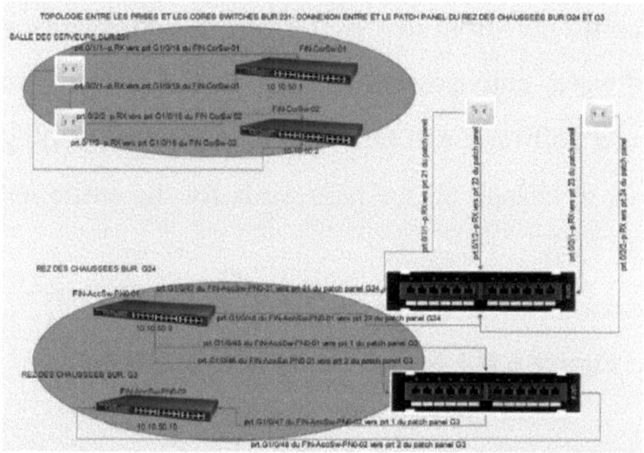

Source: IT Department of the Ministry of Finance of the Republic of Burundi

On the first floor there is another technical room in room 1-56 containing : An electrical box, including an RAC for REGIDESO power and one for the generator, an RAC for IT and telephone components and a distribution RAC for the cameras. There are 5 Cisco PoE switches for the LAN and 6 panel boards; The switches route the cables to the panel patches and the panel patches route the cables directly to the desks.

Figure 8.B.1 Floor 1 network topology

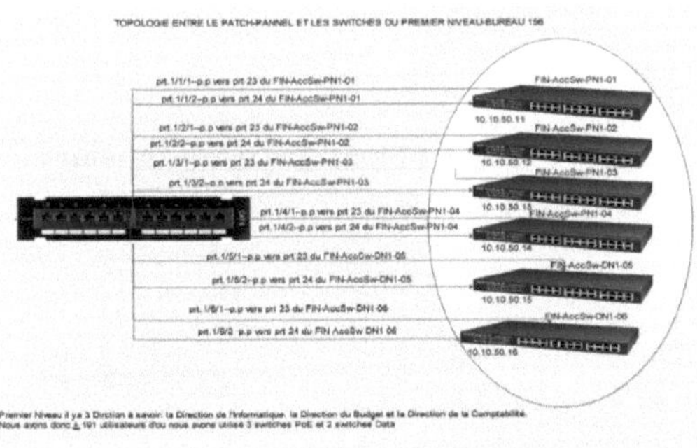

Source: IT Department of the Ministry of Finance of the Republic of Burundi

On the second floor there is another technical room in room 2-56 containing : An RAC with equipment for LUMITEL fibre optics, the internet connection for the Ministry of Finance including the LUMITEL and ONATEL connection; there are also data switches and panel patches to connect the server room and the offices on this level.

Figure 9.B.1 Floor 2 network topology

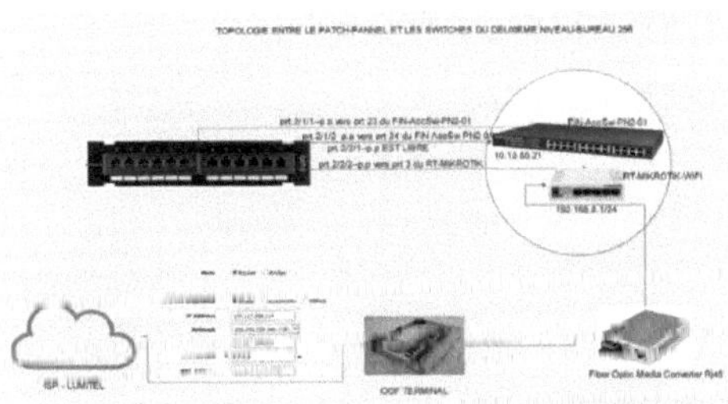

Source: IT Department of the Ministry of Finance of the Republic of Burundi

On the third floor there is another technical room in room 3-56 which contains : A CBINET router and a D-Link Switch, The CBINET connection for the sub-network of the Agence de Régulation des Marche Publique(ARMP); There are 3Switches including 1 data Switch and 2 PoE switches

Figure 10.B.1 Floor 3 network topology

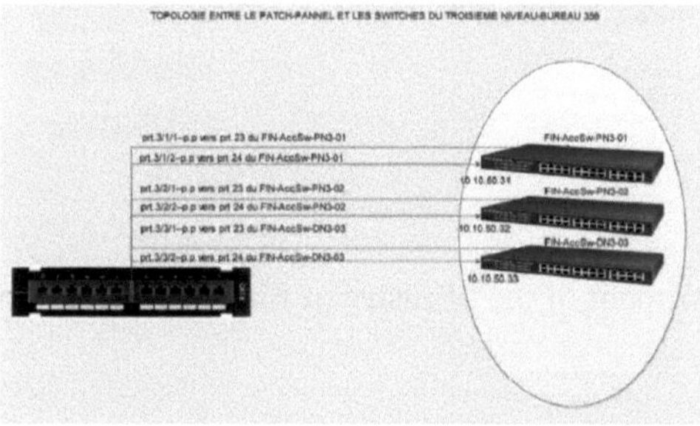

Source: IT Department of the Ministry of Finance of the Republic of Burundi

It should be noted that the fourth floor also has a technical room in room 4-56, but this is not managed by the Ministry of Finance, as it is the good governance network. On the fifth floor there is also a technical room in room 5-56 which contains a camera RAC, a telephony RAC, with 3switches and 5patches panels.

Figure 11.B.1 Floor 5 network topology

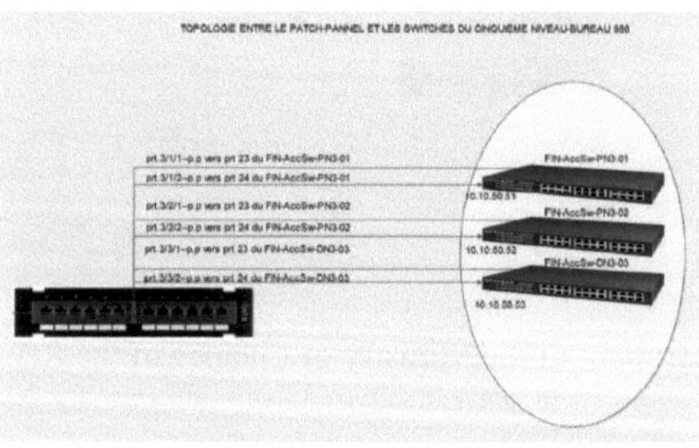

Source: IT Department of the Ministry of Finance of the Republic of Burundi

On the sixth floor there is also a technical room in room 6-56 containing: 4 servers and a monitor for the cameras; a HUWAWEI CPE for the intranet of all the departments; 4 Cisco switches and panel patches; and a digital fingerprint device to secure the door leading to this technical room.

Figure 12.B.1 Floor 6 network topology

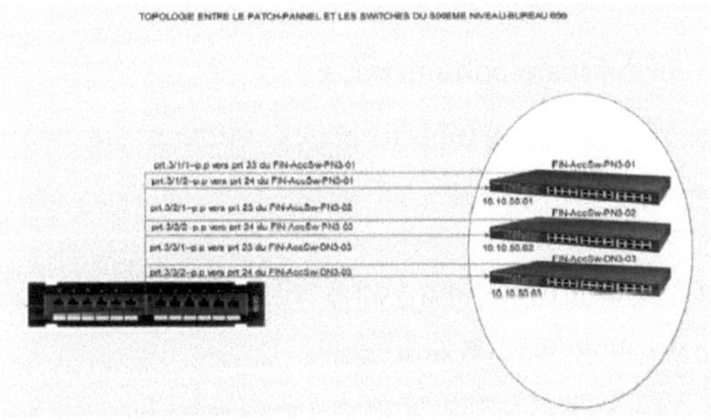

Source: IT Department of the Ministry of Finance of the Republic of Burundi

On the same floor, in room 6-37, is the person in charge of the website and surveillance cameras. It is also the Web Master for the Ministry of Finance and is responsible for surveillance camera monitoring.

Assessment

Activities Carried out

Job No. 1, Create a virtual machine on one of the laboratory machines; Install the Linux system in this virtual machine; Set up a SAMBA server facilitate file sharing between all the Windows machines in the laboratory. Samba is often used to interconnect a Unix machine to a Windows machine or to control a domain. (Ganaël Laplanche; 2010; 7) Steps to follow : Install the VMware Workstation virtualisation application; Create the virtual machine and install the

Ubuntu version12 system in it; After installation, open the virtual machine, which has the Ubuntu version12 system as its system; Check that the physical machine is in the same local network as our virtual machine; In the virtual machine's superuser mode, ping the physical machine's IP address.

To create a SAMBA file-sharing server in the virtual machine, follow these steps: After opening the virtual machine, type the following command in the terminal

Sudo i to connect as the main administrator

Then we ping the physical machine to check whether the two machines are on the same local network: **#ping** x.x.x.x

Create a folder containing the folder you want to share: #mkdir /foldername

Then enter the new folder: #cd /foldername/.

Then create the folder to be shared: #mkdir /sharefolder

You can put anything you want to share in this folder, such as files created as follows: #touch filename.txtAt the end, return to the root: #cd

Figure 13.C.1 Creating the Folder to be shared

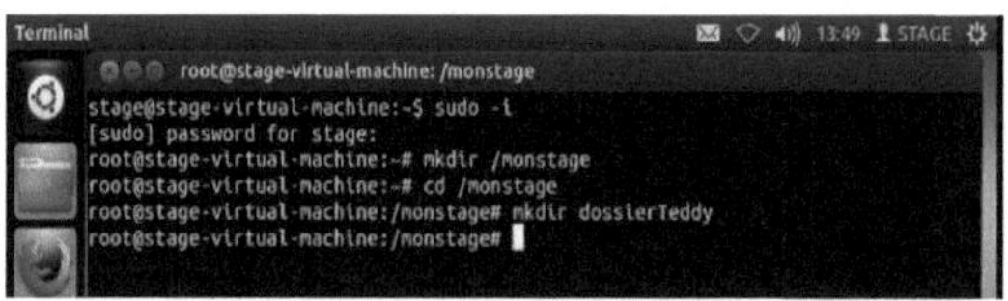

Source: Own investigation

Now we're going to install the samba package, which will be downloaded from the Internet using the command: #apt-get install sambaThen we'll edit the samba configuration file with the command :

#nano /etc/samba/smb.conf

Figure 14.C.1 SAMBA configuration

Source: Own investigation

Now we go down to the heading = = =share definitions= = =

At the bottom of browseable=no, we add thesharefolder between the square brackets: [sharefolder].

Then we add a comment when we click on the folder, we activate the read and write rights and then the path to the folder

Comment=share

Browseable=yes

Writable=yes

Path= /foldername

Then press ctrl + x to exit and validate.

Then restart the samba server with the command

/etc/init.d/smb restart

Figure 15.C.1 Modifying the Samba File

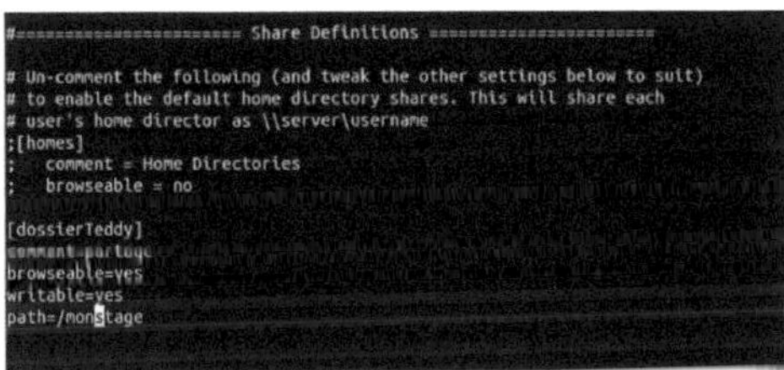

Source: Own investigation

We are now going to create a samba user with all the possible information, not forgetting the user password

#add user username

Password : password

Figure 16.C.1 Creating a Samba User

```
root@stage-virtual-machine:~# adduser deo
Adding user `deo' ...
Adding new group `deo' (1005) ...
Adding new user `deo' (1005) with group `deo' ...
Creating home directory `/home/deo' ...
Copying files from `/etc/skel' ...
Enter new UNIX password:
Retype new UNIX password:
passwd: password updated successfully
Changing the user information for deo
Enter the new value, or press ENTER for the default
        Full Name []: DEOGRATIAS
        Room Number []: +25775509080
        Work Phone []: +25771514032
        Home Phone []: +25778965852
        Other []:
Is the information correct? [Y/n]
```

Source: Own investigation

We are now going to create a samba password for our user

#smbpasswd -a username

Password : motdepassesamba

Figure 17.C.1 Creating a Samba password

Source: Own investigation

To connect to our server via a Windows machine, we'll go to the navigation bar and type in the server's IP address as follows: \\x.x.x.x then validate

To find out the server's IP address, type the following command in the server terminal

#ifconfig

We will then be asked for the samba user name and password to connect.

Job No. 2, Configuring DHCP and NAT

Figure 18.C.1 Network topology with DHCP and NAT

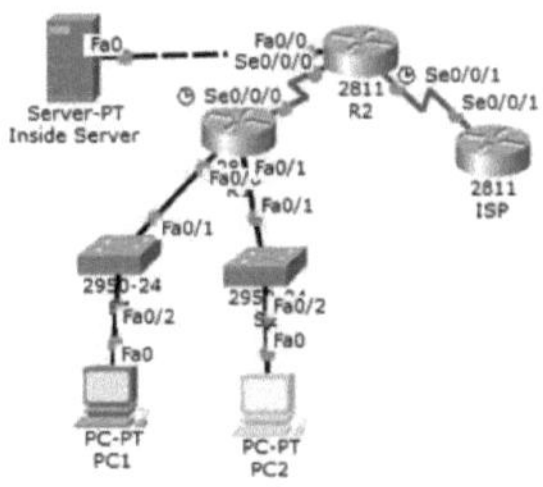

Source: Own investigation

Job No. 3, Configuring the Floor 1 network with Internet connections

Figure 19.C.1 Topology of the Floor 1 network with Internet connections

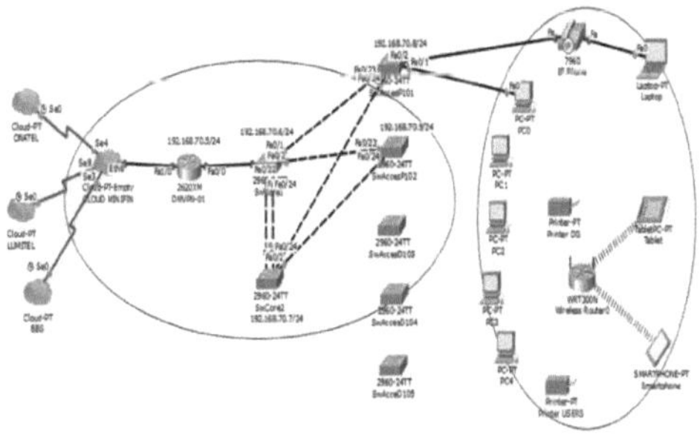

Source: Own investigation

Expectations Personal

Our personal expectations of this company are as follows:

Firstly, we would like to master all the practical techniques involved in designing a network, setting it up, managing it and making it secure;

Secondly, we want to master all the network and IT systems so that we can adapt them to the company's needs and maintain them;

Finally, we want to be able to answer any questions we may be asked in the course of our work as engineers, and be able to report on all our activities.

Results Achieved

Throughout our placement, we noticed excellent communication between the supervisors and the trainees. The supervisors did everything they could to teach the trainees as much as possible to master the field; they sought out any additional knowledge to give us and did everything they could to ensure that we felt at ease in the company. Thanks to them, we were able to understand how to behave in a company and how to do our job in the professional world. We took part in all the activities that engineers carry out in the course of their duties in the field of networks.

Difficulties encountered

During our placement, we had the opportunity to spend two months in the Geomatics Centralisation Office. The difficulties we encountered were as follows: Firstly, we were confronted with an interruption of the Internet connection every there was a power cut, even if the generator took over, it did not give us the opportunity to access the Internet until the power was restored; secondly, the unavailability of the supervisor, for work reasons, and sometimes the refusal of the head to allow us access to the computer laboratory for certain practices; The restriction of access to certain documents that are necessary for understanding the entire network. Communication between the company manager and the trainees was not very good, as the manager did not feel involved in the trainees' activities.

Suggested solutions

We're sure that every problem has a solution, which is why we've had the courage to propose the following solutions to the company: As far as the interruption of the Internet connection is concerned, our suggestion is that the network equipment could be placed on the line that is fed by the generator automatically during a power cut, so as not to paralyse work. If the supervisor is unavailable, we suggest that the company should provide a replacement to look after the trainees, but also that a programme should be set up for the trainees; we suggest that the restriction to certain documents and equipment should be less rigorous to allow the trainees to complete their knowledge. We also suggest that trainees should be given the opportunity to participate in the resolution of certain faults that may occur in the system. The company manager must get involved and consider that he is also responsible for the trainees so that there can be good communication between him and the trainees.

CHAPTER III
INTERCONNECTION OF REMOTE SITES ON A COMPUTER NETWORK VIA THE INTERNET USING THE DYNAMIC MULTIPOINT VIRTUAL PRIVATE NETWORK (DMVPN)

Introduction

Nowadays, companies have a great need to interconnect their various remote sites to a main site, but also remote sites to each other, while taking into account security of the communication. As an example, let's take all the ministries in a country that need to be in direct communication with the presidency for important communications and that need to be connected to each other to enable resources to be shared. Or shops that need to connect to the company's head office for stock management and ordering may also need to connect to other shops in the company to check product availability.

Issues

In the hope of establishing this communication, the problem arises as to which technology to use to secure the communication at the lowest cost. In the past, the only way to interconnect remote sites was to use a dual-layer network such as ISDN or Frame Relay. Unfortunately, installing and deploying these wired links for internal IP traffic is undoubtedly very time-consuming and costly. If all remote sites, including the main site, already have reasonably good Internet access, then this Internet access can also be used for internal IP communication between remote sites using IPsec tunnels to ensure data confidentiality and integrity. To do this, they need to be able to evolve the IPsec network, which originally encrypts traffic between two (peer) endpoints, and the encryption is done by only the two endpoints using a shared "secret"; this implies that encrypted networks are in fact a collection of point-to-point links, so IPsec is quite simply a point-to-point tunnel network.

Objectives

The aim is to evolve a large point-to-point virtual private network (VPN) so that it becomes a star or full (partial) mesh network.

Limitations and Boundaries

Our research was based on the communication system in the WAN network between the public administrations of the Republic of Burundi, specifically the Presidency of the Republic and all the country's ministries.
We will have to do research on the system that will make it possible to secure traffic at a lower cost and with ease of communication.
In our research, the difficulty was the lack of physical equipment to test our system, so we had to make do with simulations using very specific routers.

Review of literature

Previously, the only way to interconnect remote sites was to use a dual-layer network such as ISDN or Frame Relay. Installing and deploying these wired links for internal IP traffic is very time-consuming and costly. The VPN or virtual private network is an inter-network connection that links two different local networks using a tunnel protocol. (http://www.Wikipédia.fr) The data travels through this tunnel; even if by magic people manage to intercept this encrypted packet, they cannot succeed in decrypting it. The VPN takes IP packets from the local network and encapsulates them in a VPN packet with the source address being the router's IP address and the destination address being the other router's IP address, and encrypts the data inside; only the packet's source and destination addresses are visible. Its purpose is to : - Link 2 remote networks (or a station and a network) via an open network (Internet) by guaranteeing :

• VLAN services for IP: same logical IP network

• Extending the internal network

• Security services:

• Confidentiality of information transmitted

• Data integrity (data not modified by a third party)

• Authentication of sender and recipient (in the sense of station or router)

• No particular quality of service required (speed, etc.) - Reduced costs by using a shared network

• Using tunneling

IPsec: encryption protocol for encrypting traffic between two sites, using pre-shared keys. It is probably not the most secure protocol, but it is quick and easy to implement. (Eric SHABANI BAHATI; 2011; 41)

mGRE (multipoint GRE): protocol for creating multipoint tunnels between different sites, i.e. creating several tunnels from a single pseudo Tunnel interface. NHRP (Next Hope Resolution Protocol): protocol enabling remote routers to make their IP address known, which is used to set up the GRE tunnel with the server. The server, for its part, stores the IP addresses so that each router can find out the address of its neighbour and establish a direct tunnel with it.OSPF (Open Shortest Path First): routing protocol enabling the router at the central site to propagate different routes to remote sites. It also enables routers at remote sites to advertise their local network to the central site. Hub and Spoke: the two terms refer respectively to the central router and the remote routers. The central site served by the central router acts as the NHRP server (DIATOU DABO, GLORIA YAKETE, SADA DEM; 2014; 4).

Production techniques and design

The most feasible method of evolving a large point-to-point network is to organise it into a star network or a complete (partial) mesh network. In most networks, the majority of IP traffic is between spokes and the hub, and very little between spokes, so a star network design is often the best choice. (Dynamic multipoint IPSec VPNs (use of GRE multipoint/NHRP to extend IPsec VPNs);2) By using the Internet as the interconnection between the hub and the spokes, the spokes also have direct access to each other at no extra cost. Full or partial mesh networks are often desirable because there can be cost savings if spoke-to-spoke routing traffic can take place, rather than passing through the hub.Spoke-to-spoke traffic passing through the hub uses its resources and can cause delays, particularly when using IPsec encryption, as the hub will have to decrypt packets from the sending spokes and then re-encrypt the traffic to send it to the receiving spoke. Another example where spoke-to-spoke direct routing traffic would be useful is where two spokes are in the same city and the hub is at the other end of the country. As IPsec star networks were deployed and grew in size, it became more desirable to have them route IP packets as dynamically as possible by running a dynamic routing protocol on links; this is very useful for dynamically advertising the reachability of star networks and also supporting redundancy in the IP routing network; and If the network lost a hub router, then a backup hub router could automatically take over to maintain network connectivity to the star networks.

A fundamental problem arises with IPsec tunnels and dynamic routing protocols, in that dynamic routing protocols are based on the use of IP multicast or broadcast packets, whereas IPsec does not support the encryption of multicast or broadcast packets. (Dynamic multipoint IPSec VPNs (use of GRE multipoint/NHRP to extend IPsec VPNs); 2)

The current method of solving the problem with IPsec tunnels and dynamic routing protocols is to use generic routing encapsulation (GRE) tunnels in combination with IPsec encryption.

GRE tunnels support the transport of IP multicast and broadcast packets to the other end of the GRE tunnel. The GRE tunnel packet is an IP unicast packet. As such, the GRE packet can be encrypted using IPsec. In this scenario, GRE does the tunneling and IPsec does the encryption to support the VPN network.

When GRE tunnels are configured, the IP addresses for the tunnel endpoints (tunnel source..., tunnel destination...) must be known to the other endpoint and must be routable via the Internet. This means that the concentrator and all the star routers in this network must have static non-private IP addresses.

For small site connections to the Internet, it is common for a spoke's external IP address to change each time it connects to the Internet because their Internet Service Provider (ISP) dynamically provides the external interface address (via Dynamic Host Configuration Protocol (DHCP)) each time the spoke is online. This dynamic allocation of the router's "external address" allows the ISP to expand the use of their Internet address space, since not all users will be online at the same time.

It can be considerably more expensive to pay the provider to allocate a static address to the star router. Running a dynamic routing protocol on an IPSec VPN requires the use of GRE tunnels. But we lose the possibility of having spokes with dynamically allocated IP addresses on their external physical interfaces. (Dynamic multipoint IPSec VPNs (use of GRE multipoint/NHRP to extend IPsec VPNs); 3) The concepts and configuration in Dynamic Multipoint IPSec VPN demonstrate the full functionality of DMVPN. NHRP provides the functionality for star routers to dynamically learn the external physical interface address of other star routers in the VPN network. This means that a star router will have enough information to dynamically build an IPsec+mGRE tunnel directly to other star routers. In order to use this feature, star routers must be switched from point-to-point GRE (p-pGRE) to multipoint GRE tunnel (mGRE) interfaces. They must also learn (the sub)networks that are available behind the other spokes with a next IP hop from the tunnel IP address of the other star router. The star routers learn these (sub)networks via the dynamic IP routing protocol running above the IPsec+mGRE tunnel with the hub.

The dynamic IP routing protocol running on the hub router can be configured to reflect routes learned from one spoke to the same interface on all other spokes, but the next IP hop on these routes will usually be the hub router and not the star router from which the hub learned the route.

Note that the dynamic routing protocol only works on hub and spoke links, it does not run on dynamic spoke to spoke links.

Dynamic routing protocols must be configured on the concentrator router to advertise routes to the mGRE tunnel interface and to set the next IP hop to the originating star router for routes learned from one spoke when the route is advertised to the other spokes. (Dynamic multipoint IPSec VPNs (using multipoint GRE/NHRP to extend IPsec VPNs); 20) The requirements for OSPF routing protocol configurations are as follows; Since OSPF is link-state routing protocol, there is no problem with horizon splitting. Normally, for multipoint interfaces, you configure the OSPF network type to be point-to-multipoint, but this causes OSPF to add host routes to the routing table on star routers. These host routes cause packets destined for networks behind other star routers to be forwarded via the hub, rather than forwarded directly to the other spoke. To overcome this problem, we need to configure the type of OSPF network to broadcast using the command: ip ospf network broadcast

We must also ensure that the concentrator router will be the designated router (DR) for the IPsec+mGRE network. This is done by setting the OSPF priority to more than 1 on the hub and 0 on the spokes: Hub: ip ospf priority 2; Spoke: ip ospf priority 0 (dynamic multipoint IPSec VPNs (use of multipoint/NHRP GRE to extend IPsec VPNs); 22)

Implementation of the solution

Solution

The solution we have chosen is to install the double concentrator with a single DMVPN display. The idea in this case is to have a single DMVPN working with all the concentrators (two in our case) and all the spokes connected to this single subnet ("entity"). The static NHRP mappings from the spokes to the hubs define the static IPsec+mGRE links on which the dynamic routing protocol will run. The dynamic routing protocol will not run on dynamic IPsec+mGRE links between spokes. We have chosen the dynamic routing protocol OSPF, so we will use two OSPF areas in the configuration of the concentrator.
Area 0 is used for the network behind the two hubs, and Area 1 is used for the DMVPN network and the networks behind the star routers. OSPF could use a single area, but two areas will be used here to explain the configuration for multiple OSPF areas.
The configuration for Hub2 is basically the same as the Hub1 configuration with the appropriate IP address changes. The main difference is that Hub2 is also a spoke (or client) of Hub1, making Hub1 the primary hub and Hub2 the secondary hub. This is done so that Hub2 is an OSPF neighbour of Hub1 on the mGRE tunnel. Since Hub1 is the OSPF DR, it must have a direct connection with all the other OSPF routers on the mGRE interface (NBMA network). Without a direct link between Hub1 and Hub2, Hub2 would not participate in OSPF routing when Hub1 is also online. When Hub1 is , Hub2 will be the OSPF DR for DMVPN (NBMA network). When Hub1 comes back online, it will take over from Hub2 and become the OSPF DR for DMVPN again.
The routers behind Hub1 and Hub2 will use Hub1 to send packets to the star networks because the bandwidth for the GRE tunnel interface is set to 1,000 Kb/sec compared with 900 Kb/sec on Hub2. On the other hand, the star routers

will send packets for the networks behind the hub routers to Hub1 and Hub2, as there is only a single mGRE tunnel interface on each star router and there will be two routes of equal cost. If per-packet load balancing is used, this can lead to packet failures.

OSPF areas on star routers have been changed to area 1. By defining the static NHRP and NHS mapping on a star router for a hub, we will run the dynamic routing protocol on this tunnel. This defines the routing of the hub and the spoke or neighbouring network. Hub2 is a hub for all spokes, and it is also a spoke for Hub1. This makes it easy to design, configure and modify multilayer star networks when using the DMVPN solution. To avoid asymmetric routing or par-packet load balancing across the links to the two hubs, we need to configure the routing protocol to favour a spoke-to-hub path in both directions. If we want Hub1 to be the primary router and Hub2 the backup router, then we need to define different OSPF costs on the hub tunnel interfaces. This means that Hub1 will be preferred for transferring traffic to the star routers.his will solve the asymmetric routing problem. The problem of asymmetric routing in the other direction will be solved with a workaround using the distance... **subrouting ospf 1** command on the spokes to give preference to routes learned via Hub1 over routes learned via Hub2.

Results

Dual hub configuration with a single DMVPN display

Figure 20.4.3 DMVPN topology

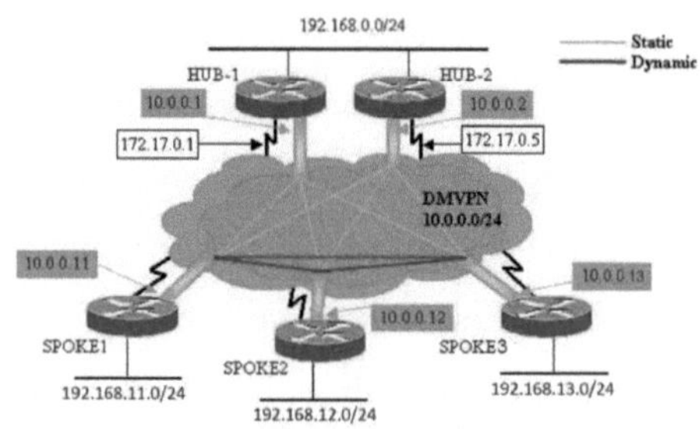

Source: Own investigation Hub1 concentrator router

version 12.3!

hostname Hub1!

crypto isakmp policy 1 authentication pre-share

crypto isakmp key cisco47 address 0.0.0.0!

crypto ipsec transform-set trans2 esp-des esp-md5-hmac mode transport!

crypto ipsec profile vpnprof set transform-set trans2!

interface Tunnel0 bandwidth 1000

ip address 10.0.0.1 255.255.255.0

ip mtu 1400

ip nhrp authentication test

ip nhrp map multicast dynamic ip nhrp network-id 100000

ip nhrp holdtime 600

ip ospf network broadcast ip ospf priority 2

delay 1000

tunnel source Ethernet0 tunnel mode gre multipoint tunnel key 100000

tunnel protection ipsec profile vpnprof!

Ethernet0 interface

ip address 172.17.0.1 255.255.255.0!

Ethernet interface1

ip address 192.168.0.1 255.255.255.0!

router ospf 1

network 10.0.0.0 0.0.0.255 area 1

network 192.168.0.0 0.0.0.255 area 0 !

Hub2 router

version 12.3!

hostname Hub2!

crypto isakmp policy 1 authentication pre-share

crypto isakmp key cisco47 address 0.0.0.0!

crypto ipsec transform-set trans2 esp-des esp-md5-hmac mode transport!

crypto ipsec profile vpnprof set transform-set trans2!

interface Tunnel0 bandwidth 900

ip address 10.0.0.2 255.255.255.0

ip mtu 1400

ip nhrp authentication test

ip nhrp map 10.0.0.1 172.17.0.1 ip nhrp map multicast 172.17.0.1 ip nhrp map multicast dynamic ip nhrp network-id 100000

ip nhrp holdtime 600 ip nhrp nhs 10.0.0.1

ip ospf network broadcast ip ospf priority 1

delay 1000

tunnel source Ethernet0 tunnel mode gre multipoint tunnel key 100000

tunnel protection ipsec profile vpnprof

!

Ethernet0 interface

ip address 172.17.0.5 255.255.255.0!

Ethernet interface1

ip address 192.168.0.2 255.255.255.0!

router ospf 1 network 10.0.0.0 0 0.0.0.255 area 1

network 192.168.0.0 0.0.0.255 area 0

Spoke1 router

version 12.3!

hostname Spoke1!

crypto isakmp policy 1 authentication pre-share

crypto isakmp key cisco47 address 0.0.0.0 0.0.0.0!

crypto ipsec transform-set trans2 esp-des esp-md5-hmac mode transport!

crypto ipsec profile vpnprof set transform-set trans2!

interface Tunnel0 bandwidth 1000

ip address 10.0.0.11 255.255.255.0

ip mtu 1400

ip nhrp authentication test

ip nhrp map multicast 172.17.0.1 ip nhrp map 10.0.0.1 172.17.0.1 ip nhrp map multicast 172.17.0.5 ip nhrp map 10.0.0.2 172.17.0.5 ip nhrp network-id 100000

ip nhrp holdtime 300

ip nhrp nhs 10.0.0.1 ip nhrp nhs 10.0.0.2

ip ospf network broadcast ip ospf priority 0

delay 1000

tunnel source Ethernet0 tunnel mode gre multipoint tunnel key 100000

tunnel protection ipsec profile vpnprof!

interface Ethernet0 ip address dhcp!

Ethernet interface1

ip address 192.168.1.1 255.255.255.0!

router ospf 1

network 10.0.0.0 0.0.0.255 area 1

network 192.168.1.0 0.0.0.255 area 1

(K. CLEMENT - F. Rico; January 2016; 6)

Note that the configurations of all the star routers are very similar. The only differences are the IP addresses on the local interfaces. This is useful when deploying a large number of star routers.

Conclusion

To conclude our research we note that the DMVPN solution provides the additional functionality to better scale large and small IPSec VPN networks.
DMVPN enables greater scalability in global or partial mesh IPsec VPNs and is particularly useful where spoke-to- spoke traffic is sporadic (for example, each spoke is not constantly sending data to every other spoke). This allows any spoke to send data directly to any other spoke, as long as there is direct IP connectivity between the spokes. DMVPN also supports IPsec nodes with dynamically assigned addresses. This applies to both star and mesh networks may require the star link to be constantly active. DMVPN simplifies the process of adding VPN nodes; this means that when adding a new star router, you only need to configure the star router and connect it to the network (however, you may need to add ISAKMP authorisation information for the new hub spoke). The hub will dynamically learn about the new spoke and the dynamic routing protocol will propagate the routing to the hub and any other spokes. DMVPN reduces the size of the configuration required on all the routers in the VPN.DMVPN uses GRE and therefore supports IP multicast and dynamic routing traffic across the VPN. This means that a dynamic routing protocol can be used, and redundant "concentrators" can be supported by the routing protocol. Multicast applications are also supported.
DMVPN also supports shared tunnel transmission.

GENERAL CONCLUSION AND RECOMMENDATIONS

Conclusion General

This work is mainly made up of details of our activities during the placement in the Network department of the Geomatics Centralisation Office. In the first chapter, which is the introduction, we gave a brief history of the preparation we received at UEA, a brief overview of the company in which we did our placement and the reason why we chose the field in which we were doing our placement.In the second chapter, we gave a full description of the company that kindly gave us the privilege of doing our work placement on its premises. Our participation in various projects is also detailed in this chapter. In the third chapter we talk a small project we carried out at the end of our course. During our placement, we had the opportunity to work on different aspects using different tools. We were really enriched by the work we did, and this had a positive impact on our professional experience, both technically and in human terms.Working with different technologies has enabled us to learn about different ways of doing things in our field. Part of our work placement enabled us to learn more about how servers work, which is also part of our field. During the rest of the course, we learnt a great deal about the design of complex networks, the study of network topology and the configuration, implementation and maintenance of these networks. We were very involved in the work carried out in the company during our placement, which enabled us to put into practice a large part of the theory we had learnt at university and we learnt new practices that we had not been able to study at university. Working in a team and using new techniques enabled us to integrate into the work group and see what an engineer's job within a company involves.

Recommendations

We cannot conclude this work without making a number of recommendations to those concerned, with a view to improving our work and exploiting certain points that we were unable to exploit.

To the Government

Making it easier for universities and businesses to connect to reliable, high-speed Internet service providers, so that they can access company resources via the Internet from anywhere without having to travel, and facilitating access to new equipment.

At the Université Espoir d'Afrique

The Université Espoir d'Afrique is one of Burundi's leading institutions and is renowned for the quality of its teaching. We recommend that it create partnerships with national companies so that its students no longer have to struggle to find work . But also to set up an up-to-date computer laboratory to facilitate practice and research in the field of technology. We also recommend that teachers should be able to introduce future engineers to work such as this every time, but also to try to guide the students step by step to ensure that the work is carried out properly and to be able to submit this project to other engineers for improvement, and to monitor the trainees wherever they do the work placement.

Ministry of Finance and BCG

We recommend that the technical department of this building organise itself to have more than 2 supervisors to look after the trainees and to have a special supervision programme. Given that they have a complex network that meets the standards of the major networks, we recommend that they accept applications for internships in this area every time, and give interns access to resources they need to develop their skills.We also suggest that trainees should be given the opportunity to participate in the resolution of certain faults that may occur in the system for the maintenance department. The head of the company must also get involved and consider that he or she is also responsible for the trainees, so that he or she can take responsibility for their development.

To companies

Given that the field of technology is difficult to master without practice, we recommend that companies respond favourably to students who want to do an internship and give them the opportunity to access the resources they need, as well as providing them with good supervision to help them gain good professional experience.

To future trainees and researchers

We recommend that students choose their placement area carefully, as the right choice will go a long way towards ensuring that the placement goes smoothly. The necessary knowledge of the field will enable the trainee to know what to ask to reinforce their knowledge, but will also give the student the opportunity to carry out a project in their own interest and that of the company.

LIST OF REFERENCES

Books and works

DIATOU DABO, GLORIA YAKETE, SADA DEM; presentation : Dynamic Multipoint Private Network (DMVPN); 2014

Direction de l'informatique du Ministère des Finances ; Document du Réseau Informatique Ganaël Laplanche ; Samba 3 training ; 2010

K. CLEMENT - F. Rico; Cisco Commands, CCNA Exploration (Revised); January 2016

Dynamic multipoint IPSec VPNs (use of GRE multipoint/NHRP to extend VPN IPsec)

Memories

Eric SHABANI BAHATI; Setting up a VPN network a company, the case of BRALIMA Sarl in DRC; 2011

Website

http://www.sp-bcg.gov.bi/ http://www.Wikipédia.fr

Printed by Books on Demand GmbH, Norderstedt / Germany